Water Gardening in Containers

Small Ponds Indoors & Out

HELEN NASH

C. GREG SPEICHERT

Sterling Publishing Co., Inc.
New York

Designed by Judy Morgan

Library of Congress Cataloging-in-Publication Data Available

3   5   7   9   10   8   6   4   2

First paperback edition published in 1999 by
Sterling Publishing Company, Inc.
387 Park Avenue South, New York, N.Y. 10016
© 1996 by Helen Nash
Distributed in Canada by Sterling Publishing
% Canadian Manda Group, One Atlantic Avenue, Suite 105
Toronto, Ontario, Canada M6K 3E7
Distributed in Great Britain and Europe by Cassell PLC
Wellington House, 125 Strand, London WC2R 0BB, England
Distributed in Australia by Capricorn Link (Australia) Pty Ltd.
P.O. Box 6651, Baulkham Hills, Business Centre, NSW 2153, Australia
Printed in Hong Kong
All rights reserved

Sterling ISBN 0-8069-8197-0 Trade
0-8069-8198-8 Paper

DEDICATION

For our moms and our mates — Dolores Speichert, Dorothy Masterson, Sue Speichert, and Dave Nash.

CONTENTS

INTRODUCTION

The popularity of water gardening continues to grow by leaps and bounds. Yet many people think they can't water garden because they don't have a pond or they don't have the room or the time for one. You don't need a pond to grow water plants. You don't need a lot of space to water garden. And you don't need a lot of time. All you need is a few minutes each week and a container that holds water.

Does the bowl
in the garden
mock nature
when night after night
green frogs gather
to prove it's a pool?
Who says
you can't make a pond
out of a bowl?

— Han Yu

(facing page) Tub gardens present alternatives for the backyard pondkeeper.

Decorative concrete baskets need to be sealed before aquatics are added.

We stumbled upon the vast possibilities of container water gardening when we were searching for miniature lotuses from China and discovered that the Chinese have been water gardening in containers for nearly 5,000 years. Even today, lotuses or small water lilies peek out of pots, urns, and tubs on stoops and in windowsills in even the smallest of Chinese villages. Miniature, tabletop water gardens excite the imagination. We wondered at the water garden possibilities—hanging baskets, window boxes, little bowls, stone troughs, birdbaths, virtually anything that holds water.

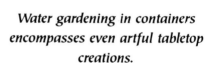

Water gardening in containers encompasses even artful tabletop creations.

Carnivorous plants expand the realm of water gardening in containers.

In our experience, we've found water gardening to be a carefree form of container gardening—much easier than geraniums or the standard fare of pots and window boxes. Everybody, young and old, green or brown thumbed, can enjoy container water gardening. It is the ultimate gardening experience for the "gardening-impaired." Just add water and keep it filled! The vast number of plant choices, from lotuses and lilies, bog plants and moisture-loving tropicals and perennials, to carnivorous plants that eat and plants that you can eat, make for unique expressions and delights. We hope that the ideas in this book will be your springboard into the creative and exciting world of water gardening.

Chapter One

THE BASICS OF CONTAINER WATER GARDENING

CONTAINER CHOICES AND SEALING

The selection of a container for aquatic plants is limited only by your imagination. Anything with a basin can be sealed or lined to be watertight. Urethane is an excellent sealer for wood products; Thompson's™ concrete sealer works well with concrete and stone; even spray urethane will seal pottery and concrete. A more expensive, neoprene paint product, available in an inconspicuous black, bonds and seals plastics and woods in double coats. Often a double layer of plastic will work for one season, if not two. Likewise, silicone can be used as a watertight glue to fit liners into containers. All these products, as well as others, are available from local hardware, building supply, and home improvement stores.

(facing page) A trio of tub gardens adorn the edge of a formal reflecting pond.

Basic aquatic plant containers come in a variety of sizes.

Terra-cotta pots need to be sealed to hold water.

Polyurethane is sprayed inside the pot, allowed to dry, and sprayed again for a watertight seal.

Multisurface sealers can be applied with a paintbrush. For best results, use a double coat with full drying between applications.

Use tape to cover the outside of drainage holes before plugging the hole with plumber's epoxy.

Plumber's epoxy leaves the tube in a soft and malleable form.

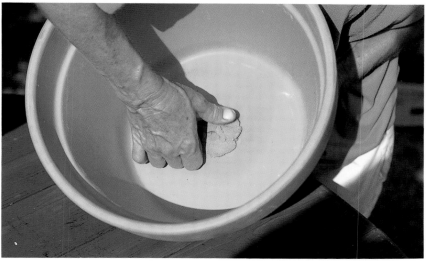

Press the epoxy firmly into the hole to avoid air pockets.

The epoxy adheres to the pot and dries to a firm seal.

Very small pumps provide water circulation in aquatic container gardens.

PUMPS AND FILTRATION

Depending on your vision of the container garden, a pump may or may not be necessary. A spouting ornament or a mini-waterfall carved through a lava rock or a chiseled soft-stone, as well as plumbed statuary, small fountains, and Oriental drips, requires a pump.

Because the amount of flow through a small water feature may be only 50 gallons (200 l) an hour, the size and cost of the pump will be small. Rena Corporation has specialized in the making of such small pumps, some with integrated lights. Other pump companies also offer the smaller sizes appropriate for container gardens.

Filtration is not a major concern. Small pumps usually offer a snap-on, particle filter screen to keep debris from recycling through the pump. Small foam filters also may be attached to these tiny pumps to provide further filtration. If the pump does not have a filter, a double layer of nylon stocking may be used.

Few guidelines are required to operate a pump within the water feature. A proper-voltage hookup through a safe ground-fault circuit interrupter should be supplied if the pump is to be used outdoors. Some small pumps come with transformers that convert to low voltage. The third prong provided on some outlets is for grounding; it should not be removed or plugged into a socket that does not fit it. Likewise, electrical cords that offer stripped lead wires, such as on 230v models, should be connected properly, with the green/yellow wire the ground and the other two live.

To power a spouting ornament, use a small SI 10 pump.

The very small pumps used for container gardens are submersible and may be situated in any position underwater. However, the pump should be properly supported; never let it dangle in the container supported only by its cord. Many small pumps offer suction cups that allow the pump to be attached to the side of the container.

Any restriction of water intake may stress or damage the pump. Many small pumps have dial-down intakes for flow regulation. Reduced flow rates can also be achieved by placing a valve on the *discharge* side of the pump or by clamping no more than half the flow of the *discharge* with clamps on the vinyl tube. Clamping or restricting the *intake* flow can jeopardize the pump.

Miniature lights are available for use with or without the small pumps.

The pump should not be run dry because motor or seal damage results. Nor should these small pumps be allowed to freeze, lest cracking and loss of the pump occur. Using black tubing, as opposed to the commonly available clear vinyl tubing, helps prevent algae from building up within the tube and minimizing the water flow.

External bio-filtration is not necessary with small container

Dry nitrifying bacteria jump-start the nitrogen cycle and help maintain water quality.

gardens since the high ratio of plants acts as a natural filter. The key to ensuring this is to be certain that the number and size of fish is appropriate to the container. Generally, you should keep the stocking of a container garden to a ratio of one inch of fish per gallon of water. Nitrifying bacteria can be mixed and added to the garden, but be wary of zealous cleaning—it takes time for the bacteria to re-establish.

WATER QUALITY

Water quality in small containers is easy to control. Water clarity and toxicity to fish and plants are the primary concerns.

Water clarity, with respect to the nemesis "green water," depends on the nitrogen cycle. Briefly, decomposing organic matter and fish wastes are converted first to ammonia, then nitrite, and finally nitrates by nitrifying bacteria. If too many

Spouting ornaments come in a variety of styles.

A bird spouting ornament can sit on the edge of a dish garden or on a birdbath.

nutrients are present in the water, microscopic plants (algae) will proliferate, turning the water green.

Still another source of excess nitrates in the water is fertilizers used for the plants. This fertilizer is applied in tab form by pushing it into the soil around the plants, or by adding it in liquid form directly to the water in the container. If you feed your plants, cut back on the amount of fertilizer, perhaps feeding smaller amounts more frequently, to allow the plants enough time to use the available nutrients before algae can create green water problems. In small containers green water can be eliminated easily simply by changing the water. To avoid green water conditions, monitor decaying vegetation, such as leaves, flowers, and stems, and avoid excess plant feedings, excess fish, and excess fish food.

A stringy, filamentous-type algae may also appear, first as a hazy green patch, then solidifying to slimy strings. Remove it by hand or swivel a bottle brush around it. Rinse the brush well after use, perhaps dipping it in bleach and rinsing again before storage. Generally, using an algicide or copper sulfate to control algae does more harm than good in water gardens. Such chemical controls remove the slime-coating that fish require to protect them from disease and parasites. Copper sulfate can also reduce plants' vigor and will kill some varieties, especially submerged plants and some tender lilies.

Toxicity in the water presents itself as chlorine and chloramines, tannic acid, or copper. Many municipal water suppliers add chlorine, which burns plants or kills fish. Chlorine itself is cleared from water by simple aeration, although products such as sodium thiosulfate remove chlorine toxicity.

Because chlorine is short-lived, many water suppliers also add ammonia to create the longer-lived chloramines. This water may be fish-toxic directly from the tap. Chloramine-breaking products do not remove the ammonia, but instead convert it to a non-toxic form. Zeolite chips contained within a nylon stocking or spread upon the bottom of the container absorb the ammonia from the water. Recharge the chips after several weeks by soaking them overnight in a gallon of water (4 l) containing a pound (500 g) of non-iodized salt. (Iodine is harmful to fish.) Concerns over the amount of chlorine in the water are negligible if fish are not present in the garden. Simply watch for any burning or premature yellowing of plants that might indicate chlorine damage. The proverbial rain barrel can be an excellent source of untreated water provided it has not been collected after running off an asbestos-treated roof.

Copper toxicity may be a problem in areas where copper is added to the water supply. Many municipalities do this once or twice a season. Copper toxicity also results from the use of copper fountains within the garden feature *when water is acidic*,

Activated carbon (bottom) removes odors and organic solids from water; while zeolite (top) adsorbs ammonia produced as fish wastes and organic decomposition.

which is indicated by a pH test reading below 6.0.

Tannic acid produces a brownish color to the water. It usually results from decaying maple or oak leaves and pine needles. Although the water remains clear, the effect may be disconcerting to purists and toxic to fish.

Another source of tannic acid may be the container itself if the container is an oaken half whiskey barrel or wine barrel. These containers may also leach toxic amounts of alcohol residue. In Canada, these containers are treated before resale to prevent their reuse in making products for human consumption; the treatment is highly toxic to both fish and plants. If the container is properly sealed or lined, the problem will not exist. Similarly, newly galvanized or concrete containers can be aged or neutralized with white vinegar rinses.

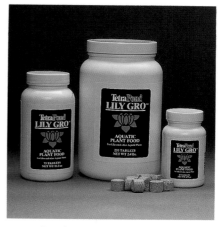

Push LilyGro tabs into the soil around aquatic plants to feed them.

FISH

Fish are part of the delight of water gardens. They're fun to watch and they perform the useful chore of controlling mosquito larvae. However, container gardens, by their very nature, sit aboveground, where air temperatures and sunlight bear greater impact. This means high water temperatures, as well as greater fluctuations in water temperatures between day and night.

Pond fish, such as goldfish, are cold water fish. Lengthy periods of high water temperatures stress and can kill them. Because the container garden kept in a colder climate is likely to be dismantled over the winter and the fish kept in an aquarium, tropical fish are an appropriate alternative. Likewise, fish kept

Flaked food is ideal for smaller pond fish and tropical fish kept in containers.

Fish for Container Gardens

outdoors in tropical climates should be suited to such warm waters. The best choice of fish for a container garden may be smaller species of semi-tropical or tropical fish—gambuzi (mosquito fish), white clouds, swordtails, fancy guppies, killi fish, mollies, platys, and Chinese algae eaters. The surface-breathing beta, or Siamese Fighting Fish, does well in the very small garden with room for but one fish.

Note in selecting fish for the container garden that they are likely to be viewed from above. Selecting slender-bodied fish such as angel fish or gourami may prove disappointing, since they will appear as little more than minnows from overhead. However, if you already have these fish in your aquarium, you may want to send them to "summer camp" in your container pond.

Container gardens are usually too small to provide enough natural food for your fish. Feed them lightly with a floating food that can be netted out if they do not finish it within a few minutes.

Since newts are not true aquatic animals, the red-spotted newt shown here (Triturus viridescens) can be kept in an aquatic garden only if dry ground is also provided.

PREDATORS

Unless you have a friendly, window-peeping blue heron, bird predators are unlikely visitors. However, raccoons, opossums, and the common domestic cat may destroy fish or shred plants. Should these problems occur, cover the container with predator netting at night or during extended absences. A long bungee cord effectively keeps the netting in place. In the case of persistent pests, a hardware-cloth screen provides greater se-

Chicken wire or mechanic's wire may be needed to protect fish and plants from predators.

curity. One-half to one-inch hardware cloth allows enough sunlight for healthy plant growth if the screen must be in place during the day. Chicken wire tends not to be strong enough to survive raccoon attacks.

INSECTS AND OTHER PESTS

Insect pests that trouble the container garden are few: aphids, spider mites, mosquitoes, and perhaps some moths or midges. The presence of a fish helps control many of these pests. Simply hosing the pests into the water makes them more accessible to the fish.

To avoid using chemicals in the water garden, use organic methods. Diacetemous earth, a white, salt-like substance, is available from swimming pool suppliers. Placed in a salt shaker, it can be sprinkled in the affected area, where its many microscopic points puncture the bodies of invaders and kill them. *Bacillus thuringiensis*, commonly called "Bt," is readily available in most garden centers. A bacterium, it must come into direct contact with the insect in order to parasitize the insect's digestive tract and kill it. Since applying the product in powder form is messy, mix it with water and spray onto the affected areas.

In the larger container, control aphids by mixing a small amount of dishwashing detergent with vegetable oil and water in a spray bottle. The detergent helps the oil mix with the water, while the oil suffocates the aphids. Once the aphids are gone remove the oil by flooding the container to prevent oxygen deprivation in the fish.

Spider mites are not usually found in the larger water garden but may be attracted to the container garden. Daily hosing with a strong jet of water will usually control them. An especially stubborn infestation may require that all plants be removed in order to hose away eggs and nymphs fully from the leaf undersides. Insecticidal soap used every three days to coat the undersides of leaves is also effective. Rinse away any soap residue before returning the plants to a container with fish. Likewise, plants may be treated with a systemic insecticide in a separate container. Leave the plants in the treatment tub for several hours before hosing them off and returning them to the garden.

Mosquitoes will breed in the smallest puddle of water. Their larvae are tasty fish food. However, if fish are not present, control the larvae with doughnut-shaped Mosquito Dunks™, floating media containing *Bacillus thuringiensis*. For small containers, break off pieces of the doughnut and float them in the water. The product is completely natural and will not harm fish, pets, or children.

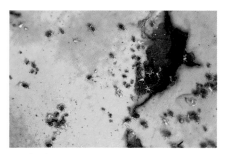

Aphids come in a variety of colors. They are drawn to dying foliage, but will also attack healthy plants.

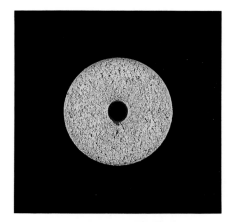

Mosquito Dunks™, a dried form of **Bacillus thuringiensis,** *can be used in whole or in bits to control mosquito larvae.*

SUMMER MAINTENANCE

Container garden maintenance does not require much time: remove yellowing or dying leaves for aesthetics and water quality; tend to insects if they appear; change water as necessary to control green water; top off water as evaporation requires; feed fish two or three pellets each or what they will eat in only a few minutes.

If the water overheats, melt ice cubes in it to lessen heat stress to the fish. Do not use dry ice, since excess carbon dioxide suffocates fish.

WINTER CARE

In a tropical climate the container garden continues with normal summer maintenance. Plants that need a dormancy period should be rested by discontinuing feeding for 8–10 weeks. Perennial plants may require cutting back. Remove the surface water and allow the container to dry down to a damp state to induce dormancy.

In climates with changing seasons container gardens need to be tucked away for the winter. Remove tropical plants *before* the first frost to prevent their death. Most tropical plants can be wintered indoors as houseplants. If they are part of a small bowl or container garden, bring the garden indoors, trim back the plants, and place the garden in a sunny window. Supplement plants that require strong sunlight with grow-lights. Supplemental light, too, is required to create the necessary 14 hours for day-dependent plants.

Patio or tub gardens can be wintered over outdoors with appropriate care. A pond de-icer can be floated in the water and

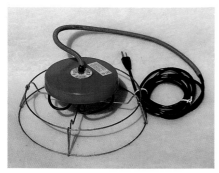

Pond de-icers may be used in container gardens kept outside that are in danger only of ice forming on the surface. They will not warm the water throughout enough to prevent freezing.

insulation (such as bales of straw or sheets of Styrofoam) provided around the container. Any hardy plants kept in the container over the winter should be cut back. Be certain that any hardy water lilies left in the container do not freeze.

Tropical 'Dauben' and 'Colorata' water lilies may be wintered over in an aquarium. Other tropical lilies must be tended as day-dependent tropicals or wintered as hardy water lilies in cool, non-freezing, dark places. Place them in airtight garbage bags and store in the garage, closet, or refrigerator. Do not allow them to dry out completely. If mildew starts to form, wash it off with a very mild bleach solution.

Winter small container gardens that include perennial plants in a large, insulated cooler stored in a non-freezing, cool area. Do not allow to dry out. They can also be wintered in a cooler with the water at a shallow level over the top of the pot. Add water as necessary to compensate for evaporation. Use an air pump once a week to keep the water from stagnating, or freshen the cooler with new water.

The tropical lily "Dauben" is small enough and its demands few enough to make it well suited to container growing.

Chapter Two

TUB GARDENS

M ention the term "tub garden" and visions of whiskey barrels or wine casks spring to mind. Typically, such tubs hold approximately 80 gallons (300 l) of water—enough to include three or four small fish and a nice assortment of aquatic plants.

Because these containers are often made of oak, they can leach fish-toxic tannic acid or alcohol residues. Prevent catas-

(facing page) Tub gardens can express your own creative touch.

The traditional whiskey barrel tub garden should be lined to prevent leaching of tannic acid and residual alcohol.

A tropical lily graces the royal palace in Thailand.

trophes with pre-molded black liners that fit right inside half-barrels. As a less expensive option, seal the inside of the barrel with neoprene paint or polyurethane. When using a liquid sealer, allow the coats to dry between the two recommended applications. The least expensive option is to line the tub with a double layer of plastic. A 4′ × 4′ (120 cm × 120 cm) piece of plastic or pond liner fits these containers. Glue or staple the liner into the container. If using a stapler, be sure the staples are above the water level to prevent leaks.

Half-barrel plastic containers are also available. Often they have no holes in the bottom, but if a hole needs to be sealed, use silicone or epoxy. Be sure the silicone is single-component, and apply it in a thin bead to produce the most strength. Allow the sealant to dry 24 hours before using. If the hole is too large to plug, use silicone to glue another piece of plastic over it. Alternatively, plastic liners can be fitted within the container.

Seal terra-cotta pots before using them as container water gardens. Ceramic pots with glazed interiors need no sealing at

Plastic barrels may look very much like wooden whiskey barrels.

Spouting ornaments affixed to tub gardens provide water circulation.

all. Galvanized steel containers, such as washtubs or livestock tanks, should first be rinsed with white vinegar at a ratio of two ounces per gallon of water.

Tub gardens are large enough to include a spouting ornament. Set the pump on the bottom of the container and route the tubing up to the ornament. Instead of drilling a hole in the side of the container to mount a spouting ornament, set it on a spike that is placed in a plant pot or use a specialty edge-hanger. Ornaments also can be supported using stones or shelves within the container, for example, a concrete frog perched upon a rock. Create mini-waterfalls by plumbing the return hose through a carved lava rock.

Tub gardens are ideal container water gardens for the deck or patio.

Courtyard tubs can be enjoyed viewed from inside the house, too.

It's not unusual to see water lilies grown in a collection of tub gardens in Bangkok.

A terra-cotta pot grows water poppies in an entryway.

*A pink Skirtbush (*Mussaenda philippica*) *from Thailand makes a lovely container plant.*

A small plastic tub is still suitable for growing a tropical water lily.

MAKING A
TUB GARDEN

Gather supplies: tub, liner (if necessary), bricks, plants, submersible pump with spouting ornament (if desired).

Bricks, with the holes on end to prevent loss of water volume, are set into the container to support shallow-water plants.

A second level is created for plants requiring a minimum of water submersion.

*Place marginal aquatics on bricks
at appropriate levels.*

*Set the water lily in the deepest
section of the tub and add water.*

*When the water is high enough,
add the floating aquatics.*

After one or two days, add fish, tadpoles, clams, oxygenating plants, and snails. Be sure the water is dechlorinated, if necessary.

Four weeks later, the tub garden flourishes with blooms and lush growth.

Chapter Three

DISH GARDENS AND INDOOR CONTAINER GARDENS

Dish gardens are created with wide-mouthed, shallow containers. Considerable variety exists in both the choice of containers and their use—colored bowls, compact tabletop containers, and planters set on pedestals. These gardens can still contain a small spouting ornament, as well as a clam, a few snails, or perhaps a fish or two, depending upon the size of the container and the diligence given to maintaining the water depth.

(facing page) Shallow dish gardens create enchantment.

The diminutive N. 'Walter Pagels' is a delightful white lily suited to container growing.

A plastic dish of lilies creates a delightful focal point.

The Eleocharis *family contains many lovely plants suitable for container growing.*

A monkey flower bowl with a frog combines beauty with whimsy.

MAKING A
DISH GARDEN

Assemble supplies: container, spouting ornament, vinyl tubing, plastic cup, nylon stocking, bricks, stones, generic cat litter, pea gravel, plant fertilizer, plants.

Drill a hole for mounting the spouting ornament.

Fit the spouter into the hole.

Remove the water lily from its pot.

Spread the lily's soil and roots in the container.

Add cat litter to supplement the soil area of the lily.

Smooth the cat litter into its space.

Set up bricks to divide container into areas for marginal aquatics and the lily.

Block the remaining space to prevent soil from escaping into the lily's area.

A proper division will retain soil on one side of the dish.

Remove marginal plant from its pot to place into dish.

Set a plastic cup into the soil of the marginal plant area.

The cup will hold the tiny recirculating pump.

The soil and roots of the marginal aquatics are finger-pushed together.

Add another marginal aquatic.

Add more cat litter to supplement the soil area of the marginal plants.

Add another marginal aquatic.

Plants, soil, and cat litter are retained behind the dividing wall.

Fill in with more cat litter, as necessary.

Fit in the last marginal aquatic.

Add pea gravel topping.

Pea gravel prevents soil from dirtying the water.

Add pea gravel around the lily, too.

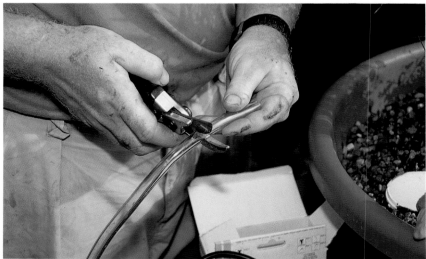

Cut vinyl tubing to a length to reach from the cup to the spouter.

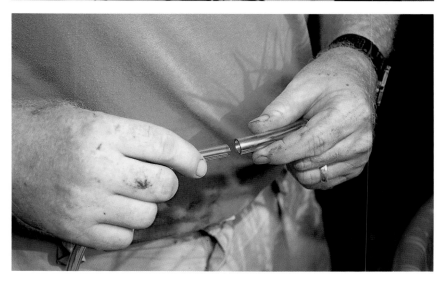

Hook the tubing together.

Connect the tubing to the pump.

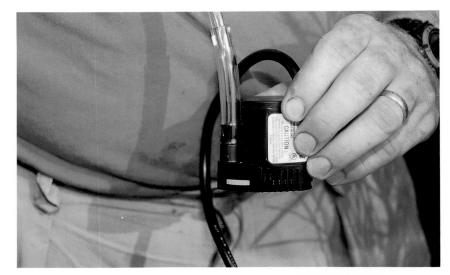

Set the pump inside the cup.

Press pantyhose into the cup.

The pantyhose acts as a particulate filter for the pump.

Connect the tube to the spouting ornament.

LilyGro is used to fertilize the plants.

Push the tabs into the soil near the plants' crowns.

Add water.

The completed garden needs to be trimmed occasionally of dying leaves and the water topped off.

INDOOR CONTAINER GARDENS

One of the most exciting innovations in water gardening has been the development of indoor container gardens. Some are small enough to set upon a desk or a small table. Very small pumps recyle water through spouting ornaments or through plumbed lava rock. Moisture-loving houseplants, bonsai moisture-loving trees, and dwarf aquatics grace the small gardens. Larger tub gardens may also be set up indoors.

For any of these indoor container gardens, low-light-tolerant plants serve best, as do tropical plants that do not require a period of dormancy. Grow-lights and full-spectrum lights enlarge the range of plants that may be grown indoors successfully. Especially in colder climates, tropical plants are a welcome treat.

Quartz and a sculptured hand are featured in this unique tabletop water garden.

A delightful cherub and water-filled shell create a romantic indoor garden.

A tropical umbrella palm (Cyperus alternifolius) may be kept year-round on a lanai.

A chiseled fountain features water in a jade bowl.

Water and animal figures create indoor tranquility.

Turtles and a three-tiered shell fountain are cast as a pewter indoor fountain.

A lighted marble ball and geode glisten with water in this marble bowl.

A pewter pedestal features a spouting fish.

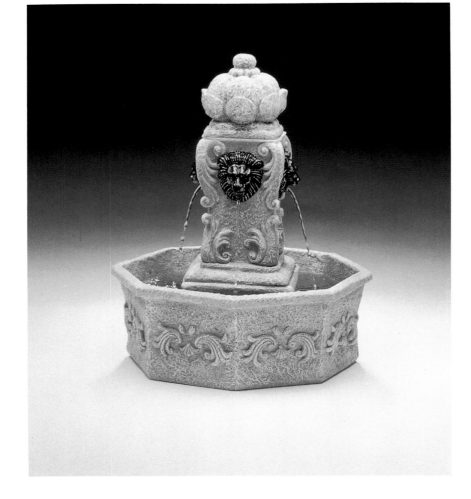

A four-sided tabletop fountain may be enjoyed from all sides.

A contemporary round dish garden with a bonsai tree flourishes indoors.

A Southwestern theme creates a unique tabletop water feature.

Moisture-loving houseplants appreciate the ample water supplied by this dish garden.

Chapter Four

HANGING BASKETS

A unique application of container water gardens is the hanging basket. Aquatic plants suited to such planting are those with trailing or prostrate habits, such as parrot's feather or ground-cover-type plants such as Houttuynia. Perhaps the nicest feature of these container gardens is the ease with which they adapt to seasonal changes; when the weather turns cold, move them indoors to hang in a sunny window until the weather allows for their continued outdoor growth.

(facing page) Aquatic plants grown in hanging baskets rapidly display lush growth.

Miniature jumping rush (Eleocharis minima) on the left and pennywort (Hydrocotyle ssp.) on the right make unusual

Lesser-tongue buttercup (Ranunculus flammula) creates a full and lush lime-green hanging basket.

'Marble Queen' melon sword (Echinodorus cordifolia) offers lovely white blooms and a delightfully speckled variegation.

Frog fruit (Phyla lanceolata) is a delightful little plant with flowers throughout the summer that change from white to yellow to pink.

Miniature water clover (Marsilea minuta) fills the basket on the left, golden water zinnia (Wedelia trilobata) blooms in the basket on the right.

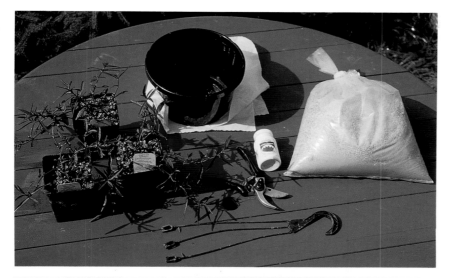

MAKING AN AQUATIC HANGING BASKET

Gather the supplies: plastic sheeting, hanging planter, pea gravel, plain topsoil or cat litter, plant fertilizer, aquatic plants.

Most hanging baskets will have a drainage hole that must be sealed for the pot to retain water.

Fit and cut a piece of plastic to line the pot, with the plastic extending up above the anticipated water level.

Snap the plastic inset back in place over the plastic. Be sure that it does not tear the plastic.

Cover the bottom with topsoil or generic cat litter.

Remove the plants from their pots.

Press the plants into the basket.

Often, more than one plant will be used in the container.

Fit the plants together in the basket.

Fill in around the plants with generic cat litter and top with pea gravel, if desired.

Add water.

PLANTS FOR HANGING BASKETS

Water mint (Mentha aquatica) blooms pink in the summer, attracts butterflies, and tastes delicious in teas and jellies.

Lemon bacopa (Bacopa caroliniana) is known for lemon-scented foliage and sparkling blue flowers all summer long.

Water purslane (Bacopa monniera) boasts tiny light green leaves with white flowers striped in pink.

Ipomea aquatica, known as water morning glory or water spinach, is known as Kong xin cai in the Orient and is prized for its tender green leaves and shoots.

Chapter Five

PLANTERS AND WINDOW BOXES

Any container that can hold a potted plant may be converted for use with an aquatic plant. Such containers may feature diminutive water lilies or lotus, floating aquatics, marginal aquatics that merely require a bit of wet soil or a couple of inches of water over the plant's crown, or any combination of these.

Using window boxes for aquatics expands these options even further. Window boxes place aquatics at eye level from within the house and present a captivating option from outside. Long window boxes easily frame a patio or garden area with the delight of aquatics. A long window box offers the option of growing both large and small aquatics, as well as lotus.

(facing page) **Planting containers are limited only by what is available.**

A terra-cotta planter features an assortment of aquatics set next to the pond.

An aquatic plant assortment in a window box defines the edge of a patio.

A plastic bench with built-in planter boxes features pickerel plant (Pontederia cordata) on the left, umbrella palm (Cyperus alternifolia) on the right, and copperleaf (Alternanthera reineckii) in the center.

After the concrete is sealed, this long planter displays aquatics.

A single planting of umbrella palm (Cyperus alternifolius) creates a striking planter.

Dwarf papyrus (Cyperus isocladus) presents a dramatic planting.

'Little Sue' blooms in a small planter with water hyacinth (Eichhornia spp.) and parrot's feather (Myriophyllum aquatica).

Remember to seal clay pots before using them for aquatic plants.

A pedestal planting features a water lily, parrot's feather (Myriophyllum aquatica), *and floating water lettuce* (Pistia stratiotes).

MAKING AN AQUATIC WINDOW BOX PLANTER

Assemble the supplies: a window box, stones, generic cat litter, pea gravel, aquatic plants.

First, remove the water lily from its pot and set it, soil intact, in the container.

Add cat litter around the lily's root mass.

Set up stones to create a retaining wall for the marginal aquatics.

Remove the marginal aquatics from their pots and press into the area created for them.

Add cat litter around the marginal plants to bring the soil level to the plants' crowns.

Add pea gravel topping over marginal plants' and lily's soils.

The pea gravel layer keeps the soil from muddying the water and makes a natural-appearing bottom.

Add water gently so as not to disturb the plantings.

Arrange the plants' foliage.

The box is ready for a windowsill or the patio.

PLANTS FOR PLANTERS

Water irises are too delightful to confine only to a pond.

The cardinal flower (Lobelia cardinalis) attracts butterflies with its vibrant summer blooms.

Chapter Six

CREATIVE
CONTAINERS

The selection of a container and its use for aquatic plants is truly limited only by the imagination and creativity of the garden designer. Some of the many options are theme gardens, topiary gardens, unusual containers, bird-baths, and old-fashioned English trough gardens.

(facing page) Sealed clay pots invite endless aquatic plant options, such as this dainty water forget-me-not (Myosotis palustris) adorning a smug cat planter.

Birds will still visit a birdbath adorned with parrot's feather (Myriophyllum sp.) and floating aquatics.

Straw pot covers come already lined with plastic to quickly adorn a potted aquatic.

Pennywort (Hydrocotyle ssp.), available in tiny to large sizes, makes a delightful potted plant.

Maryland Aquatic Nurseries' unique birdbath features recycling water through a spouting ornament.

A sealed concrete wall planter creates a unique water garden container.

Rig a plastic bag inside a basket to hold an aquatic plant.

MAKING AN ENGLISH TROUGH GARDEN

Assemble supplies: box for form, plastic trash bag, sand, peat moss, and portland cement.

Cut plastic bag open to form large plastic sheet.

Fit the plastic into the box.

Mix equal parts of sand, peat moss, and portland cement. Add water.

Mix by hand to a moist, doughy consistency.

Put mix into plastic-lined form.

Push the mix into the form.

Use excess plastic to cover the formed mold for two days.

Add sand over the mix to help hold its form.

After two days, uncover the mould to cure.

Fully dry and cured, the trough is ready to be removed.

Tear down the box to expose the trough.

Unwrap the plastic and remove.

Use a wire brush to smooth out wrinkles made by the plastic.

Apply drylock sealer in two coats, allowing to dry in between. The trough is then ready to plant.

AQUATIC TOPIARIES

Any wire-form stuffed with sphagnum moss works well for aquatic topiary. The topiary may be but a simple form in a dish or a spouting topiary within a larger container planting. Nor are topiaries limited to container gardens; in a larger water garden they can replace concrete garden ornaments.

In choosing a topiary form, try to avoid very tall forms. Too much height can prevent the topiary from "wicking" water up to the top. To overcome this problem, fit the topiary with a piece of tubing from a pump so the water spouts from the top of the form.

The following list suggests plants that may be used in aquatic topiaries. Other plants may work, too. Part of the fun of aquatic topiaries is experimenting!

Small topiaries may be used in small dish gardens.

Topiaries lend creative alternatives for water-garden fountains.

SUGGESTED WATER PLANTS FOR AQUATIC TOPIARY

*Duckweed (Lemna **spp.**), normally a floating aquatic, will root and cover the topiary form.*

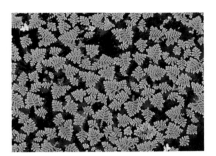

Fairy moss (Azolla), another floating plant, creates a lush topiary cover.

*Water forget-me-not (Myosotis **palustris)** graces the topiary form with delicate blue blossoms.*

Duckweed (*Lemna* ssp.)

Miniature Pennywort (*Hydrocotyle lemnoides*)

Fiber Optics Rush (*Scirpus montevidensis*)

Miniature Jumping Rush (*Eleocharis minima*)

Japanese Sweet Flag (*Acorus gramineus*)

Water Purslane (*Bacopa monniera*)

Lemon Bacopa (*Bacopa caroliniana*)

Fairy Moss (*Azolla caroliniana*)

Pink Sprite (*Rotala rotundifolia*)

Copperleaf (*Alternanthera reineckii*)

Miniature Water Clover (*Marsilea minuta*)

European Brooklime (*Veronica beccabunga*)

Frog Fruit (*Phyla lanceolata*)

Water Forget-Me-Not (*Myosotis palustris* 'Mermaid')

Blue Sedge (*Carex glauca*)

Dwarf Horsetail (*Equisetum scirpoides*)

Golden Water Zinnia (*Wedelia trilobata*)

To plant an aquatic topiary, submerge the topiary form to moisten the moss. Although soaking for a few minutes is usually sufficient, warm or hot water hastens the process. Pin plants to the form and place the topiary in a dish of water where it remains moist.

MAKING AN AQUATIC TOPIARY

Assemble supplies: container, topiary form, pea gravel, plants for dish garden, plants for topiary.

Plant marginal plants in dish garden. Shown are New Zealand jumping rush (Isolepsis prolifer) and miniature umbrella palm (Cyperus alternifolius gracillus).

Soak topiary form until thoroughly wet — from 2 minutes to 24 hours, as necessary.

Place topiary in garden.

Wash topiary plant. Shown is miniature pennywort (Hydrocotyle lemnoides).

Trim plant of excess roots.

Cut plant into small sections.

Punch planting holes into topiary form.

Push plant sections into planting holes.

Fill water to the base of the topiary. Wicking action will keep the topiary constantly moist.

Chapter Seven

PATIO PONDS

Black kettles make attractive containers for tropical aquatics.

A large patio pond adorns a Hawaiian lanai.

(previous page) Patio ponds create instant water gardens.

Patio ponds, the largest container gardens, come closest to approximating the full pond experience. Although sitting aboveground, they are the same size as many in-ground water gardens, ranging from three to five feet (90–150 cm) in diameter. Often these ponds come equipped with a premolded planting shelf that serves as a pump housing and is the proper depth for marginal aquatics. Several dwarf water lilies or a larger water lily fit into the deepest portion—usually 18 to 24 inches (45–60 cm) deep. Spouting ornaments return the recycled water or a plumbed lava rock creates a waterfall.

With ponds of this size, it is important to follow the same ecological principles of larger in-ground ponds. An appropriate amount of submerged water clarifiers assists in removing nutrients that might feed green water algae. More fish may be included, too, but the stocking level should not exceed one inch (2.5 cm) of goldfish per three to five gallons (11.5–20 l) of water. These two factors are especially important, since patio ponds contain too much water for easy refilling. If the water quality is properly tended, there is no need to change the water at all during the course of the season. An occasional topping-off to make up for normal evaporation is all that is required.

In colder, freezing climates, a patio pond can be enjoyed without being dismantled over the cold months. Use bags of leaves, Styrofoam, newspaper, straw, or bubble wrap to insulate the pond. A pond de-icer affords even more assurance of fish survival. Set water lilies and other plants whose roots should not freeze in the center of the pond or bring them indoors, as described in Chapter One.

In Bali, lotuses are featured in patio tub gardens.

MAKING A TIMBER POND

Landscape timbers create an attractive, lined patio pond. Available in eight-foot (240 cm) lengths, the timbers can be cut in half or into specific lengths as desired. The directions that follow are for a pond $4 \times 8 \times 2\frac{3}{4}'$ ($120 \times 240 \times 82.5$ cm). Adjust dimensions and depth to your needs. Note that optional materials are given for a solid-walled exterior or a pond with a flat ledge or bench along the long sides.

Constructed in the same manner as a landscape timber pond, a different look is achieved with sawn timbers.

Materials Needed

10 × 16′ (300 × 480 cm) pond liner

10 8′ (240 cm) long landscape timbers
optional: ten additional 8′ (240 cm) landscape timbers

10 4′ (120 cm) long landscape timbers
optional: ten additional 4′ (120 cm) long landscape timbers

4 ¾ × 36″ (2 × 90 cm) threaded metal rods

8 nuts and washers to fit the metal rods

2 ¼″ (0.5 cm) thick 4 × 8′ (120 × 240 cm) plywood sheets
optional: two 8′ (240 cm) lengths of 2 × 12″ (5 × 30 cm) lumber for the top ledge

Tools: electric drill, wood saw, hacksaw, hammer, wrench

1. Drill ½″ (1.3 cm) diameter holes about two inches (5 cm) in from each end of ten 8′ (240 cm) timbers and 10 four-foot timbers.

2. Drill a second countersunk hole about 1½″ (4 cm) wide about ½″ (1.3 cm) into one side of both drilled holes in two 8′

(240 cm) timbers and two 4' (120 cm) timbers. These countersunk holes will hold the recessed nuts attached to the threaded rods.

3. Place threaded rods through both ends of two 8' (240 cm) timbers with the countersunk holes on the bottom. (Attach the nuts and washers to this bottom side of the threaded rods. The nuts and washers should fit into the countersunk holes.) Set the timbers upright with the threaded rod extended into the air.

4. Place two 4' (120 cm) timbers on top of both ends of the 8' (240 cm) timbers.

5. Place two 8' (240 cm) timbers on top of the two 4' (120 cm) timbers. Continue alternating the 4' (120 cm), then 8' (240 cm) timbers. Finish the top 4' (120 cm) layer with the countersunk holes on top and screw in the nuts and washers loosely.

6. Cut the optional timbers to fit into the alternating gaps up the face of the frame. These timbers will not be secured by the rod.

7. Cut the plywood to fit inside the timber frame on all four sides.

8. Fit the liner into the frame, folding mitred corners with the excess liner against the plywood supports. Do not trim any excess until the pond has been filled.

9. Fill the pond and smooth out any wrinkles.

10. After filling, pull up the two end pieces of 4' (120 cm) timbers to tuck the liner beneath them. Use a staple gun to tack down the liner.

11. Tighten the nuts on the threaded rods. Cut the excess length off the rods with a hacksaw.

12. Fit in the last two long timbers on the top of the secured liner or install the optional lumber shelf/bench.

MAKING A PATIO TIMBER POND

Drill holes through the ends of the timbers.

Drill countersunk holes into top and bottom timbers.

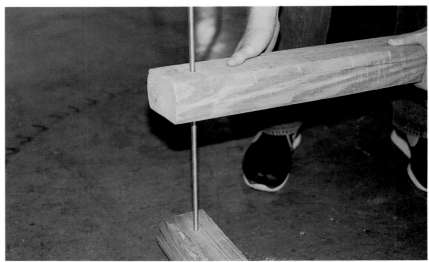

Slide end timbers onto rods and extend rods into the air.

Alternate side and end timbers threaded onto rods.

Fold liner into form.

Fix liner under top timbers.

Fill pond and put in plants and fish.

Chapter Eight

FOUNTAINS, STATUARY, AND WALL CONTAINERS

ountains and plumbed statuary are particularly effective in small containers. Traditional fountains may be used in shallow, preformed basins. If these fountains are used as a water feature with no plants or fish included, treat the water with chlorine to prevent algae growth, which clogs the fountain's outlet holes. It is often necessary to clear the fountain holes with an instrument or toothpick to prevent the spray

(facing page) Fountains and statuary combine to make unique water features.

A pedestal supports a sculpture of a boy with an umbrella surrounded by floating aquatics and parrot's feather (Myriophyllum aquaticum).

Concrete tiers, made to resemble wood, create a lasting waterfall and plant combo.

The classic pineapple sculpture serves as a pedestal fountain.

pattern of the water from being disrupted. Use black hosing instead of clear hosing to control algae clogging since no light penetrates the tubing to foster algae growth. For container gardens with fish or plants, select fountains with larger holes, a dome, or a bubbling head.

Create additional fountain options by using constructions of moulded synthetic materials or concrete. Tiered fountains and plumbed statuary may be set up as their own display feature. Likewise, wall fountains with small reservoirs recycle water through tiny pumps. These can be purchased ready to install or can be constructed of your own materials.

An interesting variation on the wall fountain is made by using common house guttering. Block the ends of each section so the guttering remains watertight. Make a hole in the bottom for the water to flow into a similar construction below it, and so on down the wall or fence, so that the final section returns the water to the pond or reservoir. Stocking these "hanging" gardens with floating plants such as water hyacinth or with moving water-loving plants such as watercress creates a unique natural filtration feature for the pond below.

Three small wall fountains recycle water through tiny pumps.

Water flows from a deer drip into a small planted wood-framed pond.

A sealed clay pot hangs on a wall to display parrot's feather (Myriophyllum aquaticum).

A large cherub sculpture delights the eye and ear with moving water.

A turtle sculpture transforms the traditional lawn sprinkler.

Big-eared and big-footed rabbits camouflage a lawn sprinkler.

A wrought-iron plant holder supports a potted Lesser-tongue buttercup (Ranunculus flammula).

An antique cream sorter combines with a milk can for a water display.

A dome fountain set within a container filled with cobbles provides the sound of water in a child-safe setting.

MAKING A
GUTTER GARDEN

Use single-component silicone to end cap for the gutter section.

Seal with silicone on the outside too.

Drill holes in the gutter section for long bolts.

*Measure, mark, and drill
corresponding hole in fence
for bolts.*

*Affix nut to bolt on the back of the
fence for stability.*

*Hold the plants in place with a
shallow layer of pea gravel. Recycle
water through the holes.*

Chapter Nine

PALUDARIUMS

(previous page) A paludarium offers a complete mini-pond experience.

Paludariums are a hybrid between a terrarium and a planted aquarium. Best suited to indoor locations, paludariums offer a side view of the pond, adding another dimension to the aquatic experience. With plants on top, a waterfall or stream, and perhaps a year-round blooming tropical water lily, scenes of the Amazon or an African jungle spring to mind. Add fish, frogs, giant millipedes, a salamander or a turtle, and a nature saga unfolds before your eyes.

MAKING A PALUDARIUM

Assemble supplies: glass aquarium, plastic mesh to fit width of aquarium, filter pad media of same size as mesh cloth, very small recycling submerged pump, support rock or bricks, aquarium heater (if necessary), air tubing, topsoil, smaller pebbles, pea gravel, aquarium gravel (optional), plants, water, fish, etc.

Cut ½" hardware cloth or plastic mesh to fit tank for land area. Cut to create desired shoreline.

Cut filter pad to match mesh cloth with a 1" overhang on all sides to secure a tight fit against the tank walls.

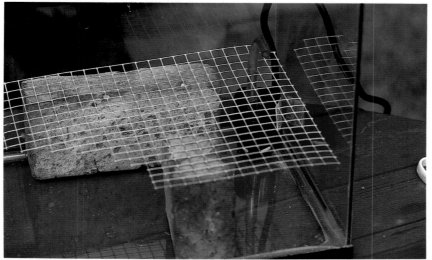

Place bricks, pump, and mesh, cutting a hole in the mesh for the pump cord and tubing.

Cut and place filter pad over mesh, cutting a slit to accommodate pump cord and tube.

Use extra filter padding around sides and back of soil to keep it in place. Add a heavy clay soil that is mixed with water to a paste consistency. Plant bare-rooted tropical marginal aquatic plants into soil.

Use same soil mix to plant bare-rooted miniature tropical water lily in water section of tank.

Use pea gravel to cover water lily soil and bottom of tank. Pea gravel can be used in marginal plant area, or plant azolla to create a mossy ground cover.

Add water very slowly to keep muddying to a minimum. (Soil will settle from the water within a day or two.)

The roots of the marginal plants will grow down through the filter pad and mesh into the water as the plants gain lushness and naturalness.

Use a large stone to hide the pump outlet. If water is too quickly absorbed by the soil or washes the soil away, use plastic kitchen wrap or scrap plastic to line the stream path.

Chapter Ten

LOTUS GARDENS

B ecause of their vigor, lotuses are usually grown in large tubs even within a pond. They also do quite well in such tubs outside the pond. Regular-size lotuses should be grown in roomy containers set on the patio, by an entry, or out in the garden. Grow miniature lotuses, such as the Chinese varieties shown in this chapter, in small dishes and set them upon tabletops.

(facing page) Dwarf and bowl lotuses are especially suited to container gardening.

Lotus 'Roseum plenum' offers a lovely rose bloom.

Lotus 'Hongbian Bai'

Lotuses are surface-growing plants that do not require as much soil as was once thought. Nor do they require the frequent feedings often recommended. Feeding but once or twice a season is usually sufficient since frequent feedings may poison the plants, as evidenced by yellowing leaves with green veins.

Planting a lotus tuber requires a gentle touch so the fragile tuber will not break. Be careful not to break the growing tips along the banana-shaped tuber. Usually available and planted in the early spring, the lotus tuber is simply placed upon the tamped potting soil and lightly covered so the growing tips are left exposed. Fill the pot only so the water barely covers the tuber. As the roots establish, add more soil or pea gravel, but allow the tuber to remain close to the soil's surface. The water depth may be increased up to several inches once the plants are established. Lotuses are actually semi-hardy to hardy perennials, but should be kept from freezing. In freezing climates lift the tubers at the end of the season and store them in barely damp peat moss through the cold months.

The successful growing of lotuses requires full sunlight and temperatures up into the nineties. Northern latitudes are not conducive to vigorous growth. Lotuses begin blooming mid-summer and are one of the most beautiful and spectacular of aquatic plants.

'Momo Botan,' a dwarf lotus, is commonly available.

Lotuses planted in tubs can be included within the garden scheme.

DWARF CHINESE LOTUS

The petite lotuses shown in these photos grow well in very small dishes.

Little Green

Hong Xai

Chongshuihua

Jiao Ying Wanlian

Autumn

Hong Wanlian

Xiao Bitai

Zijinhe

Baihe

Chapter Eleven

CARNIVOROUS PLANTS

(previous page) Carnivorous plants are well suited to boggy terrarium plantings.

Sarracenia minor, *known as pitcher plant, is featured in a pot with Venus flytraps.*

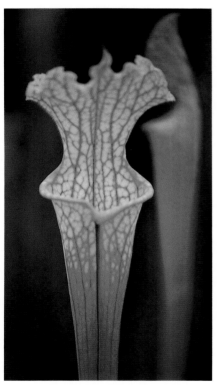

The beauty of the white pitcher plant (Sarracenia leucophella) glows in this photo.

Carnivorous plant gardens are still another exciting option in container water gardening. Pitcher plants, Sundews, Venus flytraps, Bladderworts, and Butterworts are all candidates for these moist bog gardens. A carnivorous garden can be anything from a Venus flytrap in a brandy snifter to a child's wading pool planted to mimic your own *Little Shop of Horrors.*

Carnivorous plants are easy to grow following a few basic guidelines. They need pure water—water without added chemicals, salts, calciums, and added dissolved minerals. If necessary, the plants must be cared for with rainwater or with distilled water from the local grocery store. Also, carnivorous plants should be grown in an acid soil mixture of ¾ peat moss and ¼ sand, or in live sphagnum moss.

Full sun, so long as it is not a hot, southwestern exposure, is to their liking. Winter care may be carried out indoors, so long as sufficient light is provided. In colder climates, the plants may also be wintered in a Styrofoam cooler in a protected place.

Never fertilize carnivorous plants. They burn easily from fertilizers and receive ample nourishment from the insects they consume. Among the more exotic semi-aquatic plants, these plants make for fascinating container gardens.

The unsealed clay pot allows water to seep through from the larger water container.

MAKING A CARNIVOROUS BOG GARDEN

Sundews (Drosera binata) *offer an exotic and unique form.*

1. Select a watertight container at least 8″ (20 cm) deep and 12″ (30.5 cm) wide. Do not use treated wood or unsealed cement.

2. Use bricks or stones to create a small pond area equal to one quarter of the container. Place 3–4″ (8–10 cm) of soil mix in the bottom of this area.

3. Fill the rest of the container with well-mixed, moist one part clean sand and three parts peat moss. Tamp soil firmly while creating a mound 4–5″ (10–13 cm) higher than the container's rim.

4. Plant Venus flytraps in the highest level of the mound.
Plant *S. purpurea*, Northern Pitcher Plant, near the pond's water level.
Plant *S. psittacina* in the pond's soil 6–8″ (15–20 cm) below the water level.
(This may then be covered with an inch of pea gravel.)
Plant all others in the mound and soil area around the pond.

5. Water the plants in as the pond fills.

6. Top the soil with moss, if desired.

7. Maintain the pond's water level within an inch of the top edge.

Pitcher plant, *Sarracenia flava*

Bladderwort (Utricularia), normally submerged just below the water's surface, blooms a cheery yellow.

Water-filled larger containers provide the constant water supply needed by the smaller pots of carnivorous plants.

Azolla floats in the pond supplying water to a cobra lily (Darlingtonia californica) and a Venus flytrap (Dionaea muscipula).

Venus flytraps need no fertilizing to supplement their diets.

White pitcher plant (Sarracenia leucophella) *and* S. purpurea 'Venosa' *(northern pitcher plant).*

A kiddie pool, set in-ground, provides a home for a mix of carnivorous bog plants. Duckweed and submerged bladderwort float in the pond area to help control algae.

Water surrounds a planting of S. oreophila x S. p. 'Venosa.'

A window box is planted with both ends as the carnivorous bogs and the duckweed pond in the center.

Acknowledgements

We would like to thank the following individuals and companies who shared information and photos: Betsy Sakata, of Sakata Associates; Karen Oudean, of Willow Creek; Scott Bates, of Grass Roots Nursery; Kelly Billing and Richard Schuck, of Maryland Aquatic Nurseries; Jim Sullivan, of Living Metals; Roseanne Conrad, of *Pondkeeper* magazine; Carole and Henry Reimer, of Reimer Waterscapes®; Joe Tomocik and Denver Botanic Gardens; Tetra SecondNature; Little Giant Pump Company; Rena Corporation; Firehouse Image Center; California Carnivores; Aquadec Company; Yancy Company, Inc.; United Design Corporation; Great Western Trading Co., Inc.; The Fountain Factory, Anna-Perenna, Inc.; Charleston Soap & Candle; and Adams & Atkins, Inc.

Photo credits

Title page: Maryland Aquatic Nurseries; page 3: Jim Sullivan, Living Metals; page 4, top left: Maryland Aquatic Nurseries; middle left: Karen Oudean; bottom left: Great Western Trading Co., Inc.; right: Cliff Tallman; page 5, left, top right, middle right: Greg Speichert; bottom right: Maryland Aquatic Nurseries; page 6: Betsy Sakata; page 7: H. Nash; page 8: Jim Sullivan, Living Metals; page 9: Karen Oudean; page 10: Greg Speichert; page 11, top right: Maryland Aquatic Nurseries; bottom: Greg Speichert; pages 12–13: Greg Speichert; pages 14–15: courtesy of Rena Corporation; page 16, top: Tetra SecondNature; bottom: Maryland Aquatic Nurseries; page 17: Maryland Aquatic Nurseries; page 18: H. Nash; page 19, top, bottom: Tetra SecondNature; pages 20–21: Oliver Jackson; page 22: Ron Everhart; page 23, top: Ron Everhart; middle and bottom: Kitty Poehler; page 24: Greg Speichert; page 25: both courtesy of Reimer Waterscapes; page 26: Cliff Tallman; page 27: Maryland Aquatic Nurseries; page 28, top: Betsy Sakata; bottom: Scott Bates; page 29, top: Betsy Sakata; bottom: Maryland Aquatic Nurseries; page 30, top: Roseanne Conrad; bottom: Betsy Sakata; pages 31–32: Betsy Sakata; pages 33–35: Greg Speichert; page 36: Betsy Sakata; page 37: both by Greg Speichert; page 38: both by Betsy Sakata; pages 39–50: Oliver Jackson; page 51, top: Oliver Jackson; bottom: courtesy of Anna-Perenna, Inc.; page 52, top: United Design Corporation; center: Betsy Sakata; bottom: courtesy of The Fountain Factory, Anna-Perenna, Inc.; page 53, top: courtesy of Yancy Company, Inc.; bottom: courtesy of Charleston Soap & Candle; page 54, top left: courtesy of The Fountain Factory, Anna-Perenna, Inc.; far left: courtesy of Charleston Soap & Candle; right: Great Western Trading Co., Inc.; page 55, top left and bottom left: Maryland Aquatic Nurseries; right: courtesy of Aquadec Tabletop Gardens; page 56: Greg Speichert; page 57, top: Greg Speichert; bottom: H. Nash; page 58: Greg Speichert; page 59: Oliver Jackson; pages 60–61: Oliver Jackson; page 62, top and middle: Oliver Jackson; bottom: Greg Speichert; page 63: all by Greg Speichert; page 64: H. Nash; page 65, left: H. Nash; right: Greg Speichert; page 66, top: Oliver Jackson; left and middle: H. Nash; bottom: Betsy Sakata; page 67, left: Betsy Sakata; right: H. Nash; page 68, top: Betsy Sakata; bottom: H. Nash; pages 69–72: Greg Speichert; page 73, top left: Maryland Aquatic Nurseries; right: Greg Speichert; pages 74–75: H. Nash; page 76, top and middle: H. Nash; left: Maryland Aquatic Nurseries; page 77: H. Nash; pages 78–83: Greg Speichert; page 84: Ron Everhart; pages 85–88: Greg Speichert; page 89: Maryland Aquatic Nurseries; page 90: both by Betsy Sakata; page 91: Betsy Sakata; page 92: H. Nash; pages 94–95: courtesy of Tetra SecondNature; page 96: Great Western Trading Co., Inc.; page 97, top right: H. Nash; bottom: Greg Speichert; page 98: courtesy of Yancy Company, Inc.; page 99, top: Adams & Adkins; right: H. Nash; page 100, top: courtesy of Yancy Company, Inc.; left: Great Western Trading Co., Inc.; page 101, left: H. Nash; right: courtesy of Yancy Company, Inc.; page 102: both, Scott Bates; pages 103–104: H. Nash; pages 105–110: Greg Speichert; page 111: Maryland Aquatic Nurseries; page 112: Greg Speichert; page 113, left: Maryland Aquatic Nurseries; right: Betsy Sakata; pages 114–117: Greg Speichert; page 118, left: Greg Speichert; right: Karen Oudean; page 119: Karen Oudean; page 120: Greg Speichert; page 121, left: Joe Tomocik and Denver Botanic Gardens; right: Greg Speichert; pages 122–125: Karen Oudean.

Index